DAD ✳ JOKES

THE PRICELESS EDITION ✳ ✳

First published in Great Britain in 2022 by Cassell, an imprint of Octopus Publishing Group Ltd
Carmelite House
50 Victoria Embankment
London EC4Y 0DZ
www.octopusbooks.co.uk

An Hachette UK Company
www.hachette.co.uk

Distributed in the US by
Hachette Book Group
1290 Avenue of the Americas
4th and 5th Floors, New York, NY 10104

Distributed in Canada by
Canadian Manda Group
664 Annette St., Toronto, Ontario, Canada M6S 2C8

ISBN 978 1 78840 258 3

A CIP catalogue record for this book is available from the British Library.

Printed and bound in the UK

10 9 8 7 6 5 4 3

Publisher: Stephanie Jackson
Editorial Assistant: Louisa Johnson
Designer: The Oak Studio
Art Director: Jaz Bahra
Production Controller: Serena Savini

This FSC® label means that materials used for this product have been responsibly sourced.

MIX
Paper from responsible sources
FSC® C104740
www.fsc.org

DAD JOKES

THE PRICELESS EDITION

Kit & Andrew Chilvers

Dedicated to our old mate Andy Delaney (Sand), who has never opened one of these books and has no idea we're dedicating this to him.

Introduction

Blimey, here we are again! So, here's another annual compendium of gags to keep those guffaws going deep into next year. And we thought this dad joke malarkey was just a brief flash in the pan.

As always, we'd like to shout out to our brilliantly droll, witty community of japesters on Twitter, Instagram and Facebook, who are always there with hilarious caption ripostes that are often funnier than the original jokes.

Once again, let's just have a laugh and make our world a funnier, sunnier place.

Lots of love,

Kit & Andrew

I told my son he shouldn't
listen to losers.

Now he won't talk to me.

_____

What has three letters and
starts with gas?

A car.

Dentist: Your teeth are stained. Do you smoke or drink coffee?

Me: I drink it.

My uncle was crushed by a piano.

His funeral was very low-key.

———————

Did you hear about the guy who always got angry when he ran out of bread for breakfast?

He was lack-toast intolerant.

What's the difference between
a camera and a foot?

A camera has photos, while a foot
has five toes. . .

———————

My girlfriend says I'm way too
condescending.

(That means I speak down to people.)

A history degree is useless.

There's just no future in it.

Why did the coward suddenly feel brave after touching a rock?

Because he felt a little boulder.

———————

I can't believe someone broke into my house and stole all of my fruit.

I am peachless.

> **Me: Why did you buy a fake crap for the bathroom?**

> **My wife: Do you mean the sham poo?**

Our local auctioneer has passed away.

He was somewhere around
30? 35? 35? 40!

———————

There's this new cryptocurrency
called Decibel.

It's a sound investment.

I have a friend who really hates living in the centre of the USA.

She says she's in a constant state of Missouri.

Did you hear about the giant with diarrhoea?

It's all over town.

Why do wood carvings take so long?

Because they have to be done whittle by whittle.

———————

My co-worker Celsius needed to take some time off, so they hired a guy called Kelvin to cover for him.

He's the new temp.

What do you call someone who's really good at darts?

Amy.

What dating app do lumberjacks use?

Timber.

I have a fear of overly intricate
buildings. . .

I suppose you could say I have
a complex complex complex.

———————

What do the French call it when
something sad happens on Thursday?

Un tra-jeudi.

My cloning experiment's finally paid off!

I'm so excited, I'm beside myself.

Why does Spider-Man's calendar only have 11 months?

He lost May.

―――――――

I watched a documentary on how ships are kept together.

Riveting.

The Earth's surface is 70 per cent water.
That water is uncarbonated.

Therefore, the Earth is flat.

———

My wife left me because I couldn't
stop doing impressions of pasta.

Now I'm cannelloni.

I said to the customer, "So, you'd like a cheeseburger?"

"Yes," he said. "Well done"

"Thank you," I said.

———————

I just flew back from a *Transformers* convention.

And boy, my arms are tyres.

Tomorrow, my son and I are getting new glasses. And after that?

We'll see.

My wife says the salads I make tend to be a bit on the "dry" side.

It's definitely something that needs addressing.

———

I'm not a competitive person. . .

. . . I'll be the first to admit it.

Bros don't let other bros walk around with an open fly.

It's called the zip code.

Which actor does the least driving?

Christopher Walken.

Boss: Thanks for filling in the job application form. Do you have any experience?

Me: Yes. This is my 20th interview.

Two trees got arrested in my town yesterday.

I heard they've been up to some shady business.

———————

My wife dated a clown before she started going out with me.

It's fair to say I had some pretty big shoes to fill.

What's the scariest kind of plant?

BamBOO!

_____

I just finished reading a great book about an immortal cat.

It was impossible to put down.

Me: Hello, I'd like an oxtail please.

Butcher: Certainly. Once upon a time, there was an ox. . .

My wife said to me, "You really have no sense of direction, do you?"

"Whoa," I said. "Where did that come from?"

———————

I tried to come up with a carpentry pun that woodwork.

I think I nailed it, but nobody saw.

What did Elton John say when he saw a pet rabbit at the gym?

"It's a little fit bunny. . ."

———————

Sad news, my giant parrot died today.

Mind you, it's a huge weight off my shoulders.

Teslas do not have that
"new car" smell. . .

They have an Elon Musk.

Vin Diesel eats two meals a day:

breakfast and breakfurious.

Taxi driver: Do you mind if I put some music on?

Me: Not at all.

Taxi driver: Kiss?

Me: Hmm, let's listen to the music first and see how we feel.

A genie granted me one wish, so I said, "I just want to be happy."

Now I'm living in a cottage with six other dwarves and working in a mine.

What do you get if you put a duck in a cement mixer?

Quacks in the pavement.

I gave my friend an apple, but he told me he preferred pears.

So I gave him another apple.

———————

It hurts me to say this. . .

. . . but I have a sore throat.

My wife and I always argue over the right way to hang the toilet paper roll, so our therapist suggested we each try it the other person's way for a week.

You know – roll reversal.

———

What's the difference between a literalist and a kleptomaniac?

A literalist takes things literally. A kleptomaniac takes things, literally.

I'm trying to learn the alphabet, but I can't get past X.

I don't know why.

_____

If you ever find yourself becoming demotivated, try drinking a gallon of water before going to sleep.

That'll give you a reason to get out of bed in the morning.

Interviewer: How do you explain this four-year gap on your résumé?

Me: Oh, that's when I went to Yale.

Interviewer: That's impressive. You're hired.

Me: Thanks. I really need this yob.

Why did Novak Djokovic pay for his flight to Australia with a Mastercard?

Because his Visa didn't work.

———

My wife told me, "I can think of 14 reasons to leave you, plus your obsession with tennis."

I replied, "That's 15, love."

My balloon elephant wouldn't fit
on the back seat of the car.

So I had to pop the trunk.

———————

My son's fourth birthday was today,
but when he came to see me, I didn't
recognize him at first.

It was as if I'd never seen him be four.

Insomnia is terrible.

But on the plus side. . . Only three more sleeps until Christmas.

———————

What crime do blacksmiths most commonly get charged with?

Forgery.

My friend has designed an invisible aeroplane.

I can't see it taking off.

How would a proud computer dad introduce his son?

A microchip off the old block.

I've started a flight company exclusively for bald people.

It's called Receding Airlines.

I found a coin on the street the other day, and it had teeth marks all over it.

It was a Bitcoin.

_____

When I was a kid, I wanted to play the guitar really badly.

And after years of hard work, practice and dedication, I can now play the guitar – really badly.

My boss always laughed at my jokes in the office, but since we started working from home, she never laughs at them in our Zoom chats. I asked her why.

She replied, "Because your jokes aren't remotely funny."

Why are the great pyramids in Egypt?

Because they were too heavy to carry off to the British Museum.

I asked my dad how it feels to have the best son in the world.

He told me to ask my grandpa.

I came home drunk last night, and my wife said, "How much have you had to drink?"

"Nothing," I slurred.

"Look at me!" she shouted. "It's either me or the pub – which one is it?"

I paused for a second to think, and then mumbled, "It's you. I can tell by the voice."

Me: I'm sorry I'm late, boss. I was having computer problems.

Boss: Hard drive?

Me: No, the commute was OK. It's my laptop.

Which kind of fish is made out of two sodium atoms?

Two Na.

_____

I never remember what people tell me at New Year's Eve parties.

It just goes in one year and out the other.

It doesn't matter whether you're the Queen of England or a school kid. At the end of the day. . .

. . . it's night.

———————

My wife asked me why I want to be cremated.

I told her it's because it's my last chance to get a smoking-hot body.

If you're unable to hold your bladder in the Netherlands. . .

. . . European.

———————

Have you heard about the political party that's using really good weed to promote their opinions and agenda?

It's propaganja.

I've just invented the first thought-controlled air freshener.

It makes scents when you think about it.

———————

My wizard friend asked me to proofread one of his scrolls the other day.

Well, it was more of a spellcheck, actually.

I had a debate with a Flat Earther once. He stormed off in a huff, saying he'd walk to the edge of the Earth to prove me wrong.

I'm sure he'll come around, eventually.

My wife just called me pretentious.

I was so surprised, my monocle fell out.

———

Does anybody know where a guy can find a person to hang out with, talk to and enjoy spending time with?

Asking for a friend.

How can anyone think the Academy Awards are real?

I watched it, and it's obvious that everyone there is a paid actor!

You know what they say about cold spaghetti.

Those who forget the pasta are doomed to reheat it.

I went to McDonald's and ordered two large fries.

They gave me about 75 tiny ones instead.

For a practical joke, I came into the office early this morning and switched the "m" and "n" keys on as many keyboards as I could. Some might call me a monster, but. . .

. . . the rest are goimg to call ne a nomster.

I was having some computer issues, and the IT guy said I had to clear my cache of cookies.

I've done as he said, but I don't see how eating 300 Oreos is going to make my laptop work better.

———

How do gamers like to shower?

With Steam.

Why do the numbers three and five make such a great team?

Because together, they thrive.

Before we were married, my partner used to clean up my place, and I used to clean his.

Eventually, we realized we were maid for each other.

Did you hear about the pole vault champion of North Korea?

He's now the pole vault champion of South Korea.

———————

What's the difference between a tapeworm and the Eiffel Tower?

One's a parasite, and the other's a Paris site.

It's been months since I placed my order for a copy of the book *How to Scam People Online*.

It still hasn't arrived.

My wife said she'll divorce me if I keep making puns about birds with long necks.

That's swan way to go about it.

I saw a squirrel that just couldn't make up his mind today.

He was on the fence all day.

———————

Did you hear about the town that legalized weed but banned alcohol?

The residents were left high and dry.

I picked up a hitchhiker last night. He asked, "How do you know I'm not a serial killer?"

I replied, "The chances of two serial killers being in one car are astronomical."

———————

Why are archaeologists so good at romance?

Because they have the best dating techniques.

My friend just sent me a strange text message. It said: "There's a man on the bus next to me who keeps farting."

"It could be worse," I replied. "At least he isn't on your bus."

What's the difference between a cranky two-year-old and a duckling?

One is a whiny toddler, and the other is a tiny waddler.

If slow old people use walking sticks, what do fast old people use?

Hurry canes.

When I was just a little kid, I used to pray for a bicycle, but my Sunday school teacher told me that's not how prayer works. So I stole a bike. . .

. . . and prayed for forgiveness.

I've been trying to understand why
my candle can't sleep.

I guess there's just no rest for
the wicked.

Why is your nose in the middle
of your face?

Because it's the scenter.

If Apple made a car, what would be missing?

Windows.

Where do couples go to argue when they're at the mall?

The feud court.

A B-flat, an E-flat and a G-flat walk into a bar.

The bartender says, "Sorry, I don't serve minors."

If you're ever locked out of your house, start talking to your lock, calmly and clearly.

After all, good communication is the key.

What do you call nitrogen that just finished eating?

Nitrate.

What's the best way to watch a fly-fishing tournament?

Live stream.

———————

How do two arsonists hook up?

A match on Tinder.

Did you hear about the guy who broke the world record for fitting into the largest shoes?

It was no small feet.

Why are rotten eggs like dads?

They both have bad yolks.

Tesla founder Elon Musk is originally from South Africa, which is strange.

I always thought he was from Mad-at-gas-car.

———

I told my friend that my New Year's resolution is to do yoga every morning.

"Sounds like a bit of a stretch," he replied.

As I looked at my naked body
in the mirror. . .

. . . I realized that I was going to
get kicked out of IKEA.

————————

I got my Covid test result today.
It says 50 – what does that mean?

Also, my IQ test came back positive.

Genie: OK, I'm going to grant you one wish. What do you wish for?

Me: I wish I could be you.

Genue: Weurd wush, but U wull grant ut.

My dad always told me I should marry an ancient Egyptian.

He said they make great mummies.

———————

What's the difference between black-eyed peas and chickpeas?

Black-eyed peas can sing us a song; chickpeas can only hummus one.

My yoga instructor
was drunk today.

Put me in a very
awkward position.

What do you call a sugar and marzipan Christmas cake that isn't yours?

Stolen.

_____

Why do clumsy farmers make good DJs?

They're always dropping the beets.

What do you call a snake without any clothes on?

S-naked.

What happens to an illegally parked frog?

It gets toad.

Which country is filled with bodybuilders?

Liftuania.

I met Tom Hanks once. He was so rude!

I asked for his autograph, and all he wrote was "Thanks".

Me: Even though you've been married to grandma for 50 years, you're still so romantic. You still call her "darling", "honey", "love"... What's the secret?

Grandpa: I forgot her name ten years ago, and I'm scared to ask her.

What's the difference between a sweet potato fresh out of the oven and a pig thrown off a balcony?

One is a heated yam and the other is a yeeted ham.

———

I put my phone under my pillow last night. When I woke up, it was gone and there was a $1 coin in its place.

It must have been the Bluetooth Fairy!

**What did the atheist beaver say
when he died and went to hell?**

"Well, I'll be dammed."

———————

**What word in the English language
is always spelled incorrectly?**

Incorrectly.

I need help.
Someone glued
my deck of cards
together.

I don't know how
to deal with it.

My girlfriend and I were kissing on the sofa, and she said, "Let's take this upstairs."

"OK," I said. "You grab one end, and I'll grab the other."

———

According to a recent survey, heterosexual men say the first thing they notice about a woman is her eyes.

Women say the first thing they notice about men is that they're a bunch of liars.

What do you call Batman after he's had his ass kicked in a fight?

Bruised Wayne.

———

What do you call someone who handles the finances of an ant colony?

An account-ant.

I asked my wife why we never talk about gravity.

She said it just never seems to come up.

———————

I dressed up as a screwdriver at Halloween.

It wasn't the best costume, but I still turned a lot of heads.

There's a reason Daniel Craig has greying hair in the latest Bond movie.

He had *No Time To Dye*.

———————

Did you hear about the ATM that got addicted to money?

It suffered from withdrawals.

On rainy days, my wife thinks it's pathetic when I stare through the window.

It would be less pathetic if she just let me in.

___

Did you know that plateaus. . .

. . . are the highest form of flattery?

What's the worst thing to say before a driving test?

"This thing does have airbags, right?"

———————

Today was the first time I made money as a computer programmer.

I sold my laptop.

I recently applied for a job as a spy.

They told me to send in my résumé and undercover letter.

A shark can swim faster than me, but I can run faster than a shark. . .

So in a triathlon, it would all come down to who is the better cyclist.

Last night, I went out for dinner with a boxer.

She went for the ribs.

———————

Thieves have stolen 20 crates of Red Bull from my local shop.

I don't know how these people sleep at night.

My wife gave birth in our car on the way to the hospital.

I named him Carson.

What's a cat's favourite pistol?

A Meowser.

_____

My boyfriend borrowed $100 from me. After three years, when we separated, he returned exactly $100.

I lost interest in that relationship.

A photon checks into a hotel.

"Do you have any luggage?"
the receptionist asks.

"No," says the photon.
"I'm travelling light."

———————

How many bones are in a hand?

A handful.

What's a forklift?

Food, usually.

———————

Yesterday, I went to a DIY place to get manure for my garden. They were out of stock, so I complained.

I wasn't taking sh*t from anyone that day.

I'm writing a book about reverse psychology.

Please don't buy it. . .

———

I told my girlfriend I think she's cheating on me.

She told me I sound just like her husband.

How many country singers does it take to change a light bulb?

Two: one to change it, and one to sing about how much they miss the old one.

———————

An infinite number of mathematicians enter a bar. The first orders a pint of beer. The second orders half a pint, the third a quarter, ad infinitum.

The bartender just pours two pints and says, "Figure it out yourselves."

Dad: Did you hear Facebook is changing its name to Meta?

Son: What's a meta?

Dad: Nothing. What's a meta with you?

I've created a word-processing programme to rival Microsoft.

It's their Word against mine.

———————

Why is it cheaper to throw a party in a haunted house?

Because the ghosts will bring the boos.

My grandpa was in a band called
The Hinges.

They once opened for The Doors.

———————

What do you call an
incompetent hangman?

The bearer of bad noose.

I've just applied for a job in a salad-packing factory.

The hours are terrible, but apparently the celery is good.

Where do vampires get their pencils?

Pennsylvania.

_____

All of my friends have such
impressive bucket lists.

Mine is a little pail in comparison.

If Tesla made a gun, what would it be called?

Elon Musk-et.

I saw two gentlemen on the street arguing over a bus pass.

It was a fare fight.

My uncle has two Dobermanns named Rolex and Timex.

They're watchdogs.

What's the difference between a pirate and a cranberry farmer?

One buries his treasure, and the other treasures his berries!

What happened when the comedian started telling twice as many dad jokes?

His audience doubled in sighs.

———————

What's small, red and whispers?

A hoarse radish.

Can someone please tell me what the lowest rank in the army is?

I've been trying to find out for ages, but every time I ask someone, they tell me, "It's private."

———

I told my cat that I'm going to teach him to speak English.

He looked at me and said, "Me? How?"

Did you guys hear about the underwear thief?

The police said it was a brief case.

Our computers went down at work today, so we had to do everything manually.

It took me 20 minutes to shuffle the cards for Solitaire.

Furniture salesperson: This sofa is really spacious – it can seat five people without any problems.

Me: Where the hell am I going to find five people without any problems?

**Why are there Pop-Tarts,
but no Mom-Tarts?**

Because of the pastry-archy.

———————

**Jokes about sugar are rare.
Jokes about brown sugar?**

Demerara.

I found a 55-inch TV on Craigslist for only £20 because the volume was stuck on full.

Wow, I thought to myself. *I can't turn that down.*

The first floor is going great,
but the second floor. . .

. . . Well, that's another storey.

What's big and white
and can't climb trees?

A fridge.

I'll be sharing my secret for being an amazing guitar player later today.

Stay tuned.

Why doesn't Bruce Banner tear his trousers when he becomes the Hulk?

Because the radiation altered his jeans.

I heard Arnold Schwarzenegger was just hired to star in a new film about classical composers.

He'll be Bach.

In Germany, they even have a sausage made out of other sausages.

It's the wurst of the wurst.

What do you call a hotel breakfast that gives you diarrhoea?

Incontinental.

———

What does garlic do when it gets too hot?

It takes off its cloves.

What did one monocle say to the other?

"Let's get together and make a spectacle of ourselves."

_____

Once upon a time, there lived a king who was exactly 30 centimetres tall.

He was a terrible king, but he made a great ruler.

What crime was the fussy baby charged with?

Resisting a breast.

I've been trying to find a precise definition for the word "ambiguous".

It's unclear, inexact and open to more than one interpretation.

Why did the Spider-Man in the alternate universe do better on his driver's test?

Because, naturally, he's a parallel Parker.

What do you call a boat full of buddies?

A friendship.

Apparently, 30 per cent of pet owners let their pet sleep in their bed.

I tried it, and my goldfish died.

Flight attendant: Hello, there, sir. Would you care for an orange juice?

Me: Sure, if it needed me to.

God initially intended to use wasps to pollinate flowers.

But in the end, He went with plan bee.

———————

I asked my partner when his birthday was. He said, "March 1st."

So I walked around the room and asked again.

What do two chefs do after they get married?

They consommé the marriage.

———————

What is a lawyer's favourite drink?

Subpoena colada.

A policeman spotted an elderly lady knitting while driving.

"Hey," he said. "Pull over!"

"No," she replied. "It's a scarf!"

I'm getting a reversible jacket for Christmas.

I can't wait to see how it turns out.

I haven't sold a single copy
of my autobiography.

It's just the story of my life.

What's the difference between
a dog and a well-dressed man?

The man wears a perfectly tailored
three-piece suit. The dog? Just pants.

What do you call a murderer who has recently exfoliated?

A smooth criminal.

Why do they say "be there,
or be square"?

Because you're not a-round.

_____

I got fired from the keyboard
factory today.

They said I wasn't putting
in enough shifts.

I had an excellent meal last night at this cosy little Christian restaurant near us called The Lord Giveth.

They also do takeaways.

What breed of roosters lays eggs?

Himalayan.

How do you hide a vintage video game before Christmas?

You put the cartridge in a pear tree.

_____

I called the tinnitus helpline. . .

. . . but it just kept ringing.

Great house cleaners are not born. . .

. . . they're maid.

What do they serve for breakfast
in earthquake zones?

Panquakes.

What do you call the man who shreds your cheese at a restaurant?

Not sure, but he seems like a grate guy.

Did you hear the Incredible Hulk
has started recycling?

He's really going green.

I saw my son eating chocolate, even
after I had confiscated all his Halloween
candy. I asked him where he got it from.

He said, "I always have a few Twix
up my sleeve."

What's a thousand times better
than Instagram?

Instakilogram.

———————

My girlfriend treats me like a god.

She ignores my existence and only talks
to me when she needs something.

I told the waiter my steak was bad.

He picked it up, slapped it and threw it back down, then said, "If it gives you any more trouble, just let me know."

What kind of fruit do ghosts like?

Boo berries.

Did you hear about the criminal who was aroused by semantics?

He got off on a technicality.

What do laxatives and seat cushions have in common?

They're both stool softeners.

_____

Which body part is most reliable?

Well, you can always count on your fingers.

I heard you can get lawyers at IKEA now.

They're very affordable, but you have to build your own case.

———————

I recently came into a lot of money. . .

. . . and that's why I got fired from the bank.

What do they call the employee of the month at the crematorium?

The top urner.

———

My wife left me for another man. All that lies ahead now is a miserable, pointless, lonely life.

And while he's going through that, I'll be down the pub with my mates every night.

What do you call a Swedish telemarketer?

A Scamdinavian.

———————

My next-door neighbour just knocked on my door with her dinner in her hands.

It turns out Facebook and Instagram are down, and she just wanted me to see what she was eating.

> **Sarcasm doesn't get you anywhere.**

> **Well, it got me to the Sarcasm World Championships in Mexico '98.**

> **Really?**

> **No. . .**

What kind of horses come out after the sun sets?

Nightmares.

———

I had the rudest, slowest, nastiest cashier today!

I guess it's my own fault for using the self-checkout lane.

A ghost who used to haunt me as
a kid visited me again last night.

Gave me déjà BOO!

What do you call a fish without an eye?

Fsh.

Where do you find a crab with no legs?

Exactly where you left it.

Penguins produce an oil that helps
their feathers retain heat.

So it's true what they say:
the oily bird gets the warm.

―――――――

I heard that you should always look into
a mirror before making a big decision.

It helps you reflect.

I took all my savings out of the bank and put the cash on a boat.

I feel much better now that my money is offshore.

―――――――

Why do fishermen do well at geometry?

They are good anglers!

If you're a comedian, never do
a show for ghosts.

There's a 100 per cent chance
you'll get booed off the stage.

———

I'm writing a book about all the things
I should be doing with my life.

It's an oughta-biography.

Have you heard about the big dental convention they're holding in Nevada?

It's called Floss Vegas.

———

I've just invented a machine that can create facsimiles of prosthetic appendages.

Essentially, it's a faux-toe-copier.

I used to read comic books,
but I stopped.

They're just far too graphic.

With great power comes. . .

. . . a great electricity bill.

I just broke up with my mathematician girlfriend.

She was still obsessed with her x.

———

I once dated a magazine collector.

Let's just say he had issues.

I threw a ball for my dog.

It's a bit extravagant, I know, but it was his birthday – and he looks great in a tuxedo.

To whoever stole my cow:

my beef is with you, sir!

———————

Sadly, the guy who invented the fruit smoothie has passed away.

He's being berried on Friday.

Why didn't the skeleton cross the road?

Because he had no stomach for it.

I loaned my grandfather clock to my friend and he still hasn't returned it.

He owes me big time.

_____

That guy stole my place in the queue.

I'm after him now.

When you're waiting for the waiter. . .

. . . you *become* the waiter.

Where do bicycles go for a drink around here?

Handle bars.

What do a tight pair of underpants and a small terraced house have in common?

No ballroom.

———————

What do you call a bloodsucking tax specialist?

Account Dracula.

Do you know any good corn jokes?

I'm all ears.

———————

What do you call an anti-vax nanny?

Mrs Doubt Pfizer.

I went to see a psychic, but she was in a bad mood. Then I tried a clairvoyant, but he was really grumpy.

I'm just trying to find a happy medium.

We started a band and called it Books.

We're hoping it means no one will judge us by our covers.

_____

You shouldn't eat more than 239 beans in one sitting.

One more would be too farty!

I was going to tell a joke about sodium and oxygen. . .

. . . but I'm afraid I'd get a violent reaction.

My brother just started dating a girl called Rosemary.

I don't know what he season her.

I recently befriended a ghost who keeps wheezing all the time.

I named him Gasper.

———————

A mate of mine just got a smart washing machine that's Wi-Fi enabled.

I told him not to let it on social media, or it'll air all his dirty laundry.

What do you call an ancient Greek who is just a bit, well, average?

Mediocrates.

I saw a bunch of batteries gathered around in a circle.

I guess they were having an AA meeting.

———

What do cars spread on their toast?

Traffic jam.

My wife left me
because I didn't
do enough chores
around the house.

I'm devastated. . .
I didn't do much
to deserve it.

**How did the phone propose
to his girlfriend?**

He gave her a ring.

_____

**What's the term for when a person
dies and comes back as a hillbilly?**

Reintarnation.

What did Arnold Schwarzenegger say when his wife asked him why he hadn't updated to Windows 10?

"I still love Vista, baby!"

My friend stole one of my board games, so I took one of theirs for revenge.

They took a *Risk*, but now they don't have a *Clue*.

My son asked me why I was washing the dishes while sitting down.

I told him it's because I can't stand doing it.

———————

Did you know that bees are actually allergic to pollen?

It makes them break out in hives.

I started my own all-natural fertilizer company recently.

I guess that makes me an entre-manure!

———————

Why do computer programmers prefer to work the dark?

Because the light attracts bugs.

What car does a Jedi drive?

A Toyoda.

———————

What do you call a Grim Reaper with hearing problems?

Deaf.

What did the judge say to the dentist?

"Do you swear to pull the tooth, the whole tooth and nothing but the tooth?"

———

What do you call a one-legged hippo?

A hoppo.

Robber: Give me all your money, or you’re geography!

Bank manager: Wait, what? Don’t you mean history?

Robber: Don’t change the subject!

**Why did the Cyclops stop teaching
at the school?**

Because he only had one pupil.

_____

**Why don't pirates like travelling
on mountain roads?**

'Scurvy.

Who's the genius that decided to call it "emotional baggage" and not "grief case"?

My partner just broke up with me. He says my life revolves around football, and he's sick of it. I'm quite upset.

We were together for seven seasons.

———————

My dad was down at the auto dealership, looking at potential choices. Examining one of the vehicles, he asked, "Hmm. . . cargo space?"

The salesperson said, "Um. Car no do that. Car go road."

**Where do maths teachers go
on vacation?**

Times Square.

I'd like to have kids one day. . .

**I don't think I could stand them any
longer than that, though.**

I'm opening a chain of Elvis-themed steak restaurants. . .

They'll be for people who love meat tender.

Where do wolves like to stay while on vacation?

At the Howl-iday Inn.

Apparently, to start a zoo you need at least two pandas, a grizzly and three polars.

It's the bear minimum.

———

What's the opposite of Antarctica?

Uncle Arctica.

I mistakenly took a ten-minute video of my shoes yesterday.

It was an accident, but I actually got some pretty good footage.

I'm thinking of removing my spine.

I think it's the only thing holding me back.

———————

The CEO of IKEA was just elected

Prime Minister of Sweden.

The first thing he'll need to do is to assemble his cabinet.

Kid: Dad, do trees poop?

Dad: Where do you think number two pencils come from?

I asked my dog, "What's
two minus two?"

He said nothing.

———————

Tablets were replaced by scrolls, then
scrolls were replaced by books. . .

. . . and now we scroll through books
on tablets.

For her birthday, I took my wife to an orchard, and we stood there looking at the trees for half an hour.

Apparently, it was not the kind of Apple Watch she was expecting.

Why was the moon detained?

Lunacy.

My therapist told me to write letters to everyone who's hurt me, then burn them.

I've done that, but what do I do with the letters?

———————

My wife threatened to leave me if I didn't stop making *Star Wars* puns.

I guess divorce is strong with this one. . .

My six-year-old is the only one in his class who doesn't believe in Santa.

He's a rebel without a Claus.

———————

Fun fact: oxygen solidifies at -218.79°C.

That's *really* cool.

> **Hello, is that the paranoia hotline?**

> **How did you get this number?!**

When my dad was unemployed, he used to hide money in the bushes in our garden.

He went on to become a successful hedge-fund manager.

My wife said if I bought her one more stupid gift, she would burn it.

So I bought her a candle.

I just got a job in a factory making plastic Draculas.

There are only two of us working on the production line, so I have to make every second count.

**What has two grey legs
and two brown legs?**

An elephant with diarrhoea.

**How do two French guys share
files electronically?**

They use a Pierre-to-Pierre network.

Did you hear about the mechanic
who fell asleep under the car?

He woke up oily in the morning.

A man walks into the doctor's office
with a frog on his head.

The doctor says, "Can I help you?"

"Yes please," says the frog. "Can you cut
this wart off my rear end?"

Who hides in the bathroom at parties?

The party-pooper.

_____

What do you call a sexy flying monkey?

A hot air baboon.

Waiter: All finished, sir? How did you find your steak?

Dad: I just looked next to the potatoes, and there it was.

My inflatable house got a puncture last night.

Now I'm living in a flat.

_____

Why should you never brush your teeth with your left hand?

Because a toothbrush works better.

I returned my lizard to the pet store because he wouldn't stop telling dad jokes.

"That's not a lizard," the shop assistant told me. "That's a stand-up chameleon."

———

15 + 15 = 30.

16 + 16 = 30 too.

Who were the greenest Presidents in US history?

The Bushes.

David Beckham gets in a taxi and realizes the driver is staring at him in the rear-view mirror.

After two minutes without moving, the driver says, "Go on, then. Give me a clue."

Beckham replies, "OK, I played for Manchester United and England and married a Spice Girl – is that enough?"

"No, David," says the driver. "I meant where are you going?"

———

Why didn't Hans Solo enjoy his steak dinner?

It was Chewie.

I tried flushing my Dutch slippers down the toilet.

Now the drain is all clogged up.

————————

What do you call the sexuality where you're attracted to both men and women, but neither is attracted to you?

Bi-yourself.

I had a broken neck last year, which wasn't much fun.

But at least now I can look back and laugh.

———————

If you think swimming with dolphins is expensive, you should try swimming with sharks.

It cost me an arm and a leg!

**What did the shipmates find
in the toilet?**

The captain's log.

———————

What do you call sweaty boobs?

Humidititties.

I've got a condition that causes me to make terrible puns.

It's a dad-ly disease.

————————

I went to a bookstore and saw a book called *How to Solve 50 Per Cent of Your Problems*. I bought two copies.

What did the surgeon say to the patient who insisted on closing his own incision?

"Suture self."

**What's the difference between
a bowl of mouldy lettuce and
a depressing song?**

**One is a bad salad, and the other
is a sad ballad.**

**I was going to propose to my girlfriend,
but my dog ate the ring.**

Now it's a diamond in the ruff.

Why do librarians hate tennis?

Too much racket.

———————

The other day, my wife asked me how I became so damn good at making love.

I told her she should thank all the women who came before her.

Daughter: Dad, what's your password?

Dad: MickeyMinnieGoofyDonaldPlutoHueyLouieDeweyDublin.

Daughter: Wow, why's it so long?

Dad: Because they said it had to contain at least eight characters and at least one capital.

You should always fear a pirate duck.

He has the power to unleash
the quackin.

———————

I tried to bring my oversized board
game on to the plane with me, but
I wasn't allowed.

They said the Risk was just too big.

What do you call a castrated unicorn?

A eunuchorn.

_____

That's the tenth passenger today who's called me a terrible bus driver.

I don't know where these people get off.

What tastes better than it smells?

A tongue!

My girlfriend complains that I don't smile anymore.

Well, she's the one who wanted a serious relationship!

Archaeologists are holding a party to celebrate unearthing the largest ever dinosaur tibia.

It's going to be quite the shindig.

When I was young, my mum used to tear out the last page of all my comics. She wouldn't tell me why.

I had to draw my own conclusions.

———

A boy asked his Bitcoin-investing dad for one Bitcoin for his birthday.

His dad said, "What? $15,554? $14,354 is a lot of money! What do you need $16,782 for, anyway?"

Which Disney princess spends most of her day on dating apps?

Tinderella.

What's the difference between a cat and a frog?

A cat has nine lives, but the frog croaks every night.

At the weekend, I like to play chess with elderly men in the park.

But it's becoming increasingly difficult to find exactly 32 of them.

———————

My wife and I were really happy for 20 years.

Then we met.

What's the most desired summer body this year?

The antibody.

———

Two sausages are sizzling away in a pan.

The first one says, "Oh, man, it's hot in here!"

The second one says, "AHHHH!!! A TALKING SAUSAGE!!!"

What do you call a kangaroo wearing a sweater?

A woolly jumper.

My next-door neighbour and I were very good friends, so we decided to share our water supply. . .

. . . because we got along well.

I have the attention of a goldfish.

Seriously, it's been watching me for hours.

What did you get your son for his birthday?

I got him an alarm clock that swears at him instead of beeping.

Wow, sounds like he's in for a rude awakening.

Which insect is high in cholesterol?

A butterfly.

___

I don't understand all this controversy around cloning.

Clones are people two.

My grandfather was terrible until I had my first child.

Now he's a great-grandfather.

———

I grilled a chicken for two hours.

It still wouldn't tell me why it crossed the road.

I was all set to become one of the world's greatest mountain climbers. . .

. . . but I peaked too early.

———————

My last girlfriend said I was unnecessarily mysterious.

Or did she?

I couldn't sleep last night,
so I read a dictionary.

By 3am, I was past caring.

———————

One of my daughters wants
to marry the postman. . .

. . . but I won't letter!

Farmers are leaving Facebook in their droves.

Every time they put down a post, somebody takes a fence.

———————

What flavour is the toothpaste in jail?

Imprisonmint.

My friend once used laughing gas as deodorant.

He smelled funny the whole day.

———

My mate broke his leg, so I wrote "You are stupid" on his cast.

I was just adding insult to injury.

Pandora's box wasn't actually a box.

In fact, all that trouble started because it was ajar.

———————

How long is one minute?

It depends what side of the bathroom door you're on.

I once dated a condemned witch.

There was a lot at stake in the relationship, but now she's just an old flame.

———

My friend Tony asked me not to say his name backwards.

I asked, "Y not?"

Why did the mystic refuse Novocaine?

He wanted to transcend dental medication.

Doctor: How have you been since our last appointment? Have you managed to reduce the cigarettes you smoke?

Me: Oh, yes. They're definitely shorter by the time I've finished them.

My mum is a radiologist. She met my dad when he came in for an X-ray.

I wonder what she saw in him.

———

I'm trying to organize a hide-and-seek tournament.

But good players are really hard to find.

What do you get when you mix a penis, a potato and a boat?

A dick-tator-ship.

Someone called me lazy today.

I almost replied. . .

After I went to the dentist, I headed to the studio and recorded a gospel album. My mouth was still numb, so I was drooling the whole time.

The album's called *Songs of Salivation*.

———————

Did you hear the semicolon got arrested?

It got two back-to-back sentences.

A lot of people can't tell the difference between entomology and etymology.

I can't find the words for how much this bugs me.

My psychiatrist says I have an unhealthy obsession with revenge.

We'll see about that. . .

A man is told that his local bank is currently offering mortgages with no interest. He heads along to the branch to find out more.

"Hello," he says. "I'm here to enquire about your mortgages."

The bank manager replies, "I don't really care."

What's worse than raining cats and dogs?

Hailing taxis.

Me: Hi, can I borrow *Batman Forever*?

Video-store manager: No, you'll have to bring it back tomorrow.

I've decided to name my son Mark.

That way, when I die, I'll be able to say I left a Mark on this world.

———

What did the farmer say when all of his haystacks were stolen?

"This is the last straw!"

I really wanted to become a monk.

But I never got the chants.

My doctor has advised me to stop drinking. It's clearly time for me to make a massive change.

It's going to be tough; I've been with that doctor for 15 years.

What do you call a knight who loves to scare people?

Sir Prise.

I always take my problems to Tommy. Hilfiger something out.

———————

Why do cow-milking stools only have three legs?

Because the cow has the udder.

Therapist: What brings you in today?

Me: I have a terrible fear of tsunamis.

Therapist: How bad is it?

Me: It comes in waves.

Does anyone know any good sword-fighting puns?

I'm trying to think of any words that have a duel meaning.

———————

After staying silent for a long time, I finally told my hot co-worker how I felt.

They felt the same way.

So, I turned on the air conditioner.

I'm a fisherman, and I'm dating
a mermaid.

I met her online.

———————

I quit my job as a scuba-diving instructor
after giving my first lesson.

Deep down, I knew it wasn't for me.

I finally finished childproofing my home, but I didn't do a very good job.

My kids are still able to get into the house.

I'm in a band called Dyslexia.

We've just released our compilation album, *Greatest sHit*.

I told my son to go and find out what *"nada"* means in English.

He came back with nothing.

A door-to-door salesperson knocks on the front door of a house.

It's answered by a 12-year-old, holding a glass of cognac and smoking a cigar.

The salesperson asks, "Are your parents home?"

The kid replies, "What do you think?"

———

When Bill and Melinda Gates got divorced. . .

. . . Melinda got the house, but Bill kept the Windows.

Breaking news: historians believe that they've uncovered a cache of pencils that once belonged to William Shakespeare.

A spokesperson said, "They're so badly chewed on the ends, we can't tell if they're 2B or not 2B."

———————

My friends love scaring the crap out of me.

With friends like that, who needs enemas?

Doctor: How's your broken arm feeling?

Me: Pretty sore.

Doctor: Do you think painkillers will help?

Me: It wouldn't hurt.

My friend was bragging that his new 3D printer can print a gun.

Big deal. I've had a Canon printer for years.

Once again, I've entered our town's annual Tightest Hat Competition.

This year, I'm really hoping I can pull it off.

What's the worst thing about having a job at the unemployment office?

If you get fired, you still have to show up the next day.

———————

I went to an Indian restaurant and asked for some garlic bread.

But they had naan.

I'm having a hell of a time getting this yoga instructor to leave my house.

Every time I ask her to leave, she just says, "Namaste."

———————

What do you call a cruise ship filled with skilled artisans?

Great Craftsman Ship.

Why isn't 24 July a holiday?

Are we really expected to work 24/7?

———————

How do you make antifreeze?

You take away her blanket.

I saw a deer on the way to work this morning.

How do you know it was on its way to work?

I've trained my dog to go and fetch me a bottle of wine.

He's a Bordeaux collie.

_____

Never scream into a colander.

You'll strain your voice.

My teacher asked me to make up a sentence using the words "defence", "defeat" and "detail".

I wrote: "When a horse jumps over defence, defeat go first, then detail."

Our doorbell rang and my son called to me, "Dad, there's a salesperson here with a moustache!"

I yelled back, "Tell him I've already got one!"

My wife asked if I think our kids are spoiled.

"No," I said. "I think most kids smell that way!"

Just had a police officer at the door saying he was looking for a man with one eye.

I told him to use both: he'd probably find him a lot quicker that way.

I asked my dad why he decided to buy a boat.

He said, "There was a sail."

I gave my daughter a watch for her birthday.

When she showed it to the next-door neighbour, he said, "That's a pretty new watch you've got there! Does it tell you the time?"

She laughed and said, "No, this is an old-fashioned watch! You have to look at it."

Why do people wear shamrocks on St Patrick's Day?

Real rocks are too heavy.

What's the highest rank in the popcorn army?

Kernel.

A platypus walks into a bar owned by a duck.

The platypus finishes his drink and asks to pay.

Duck billed platypus.

What do you call a walking mosquito?

An itch-hiker.

_____

What does a clam do on his birthday?

He shell-ebrates.

If H20 is on the inside of a fire hydrant, what's on the outside?

K9P.

I got fired from Uber.

Apparently, they didn't like it when I went the extra mile.

Why is the letter "a" like a flower?

Because a "b" comes after it!

———

What is the smelliest kind of ox?

A buttocks.

My wife accused me of hating her family.

"That's not true," I told her. "Your mother-in-law is way better than mine!"

What happens when you put your hand in a blender?

You get a handshake.

_____

What is a doctor who specializes in Adam's apples called?

A guyneckologist.

What type of haircut does Steven Spielberg get?

The director's cut.

I recently joined a support group for people who talk a lot.

We call ourselves On and On Anon.

Hey, Dad, what does déjà vu mean?

I have a feeling you've asked me this before.

Since Facebook claims ownership of everything you post on their website. . .

. . . I've decided to start uploading my electricity bills.

_____

I decided to stop walking under billboards after one collapsed on top of me.

I took it as a sign from above.

What did the movie director say before shooting a dangerous stunt scene?

"It's a take I'm willing to risk."

———————

My girlfriend left me while I was crying in the bathroom with constipation.

She told me that I was so full of it.

It was the hardest dump I ever took.

How many wives can a monk have?

Nun.

I finally found a genie in a bottle!

I asked him if it would be possible to change French positives to Spanish.

He replied, *"Oui* shall *sí."*

What do you call someone who can't stop watching films with strong female leads?

A heroine addict.

How did the computer eat its supper?

In megabytes.

Which bones drive other bones to work?

The metacarpools.

I looked out of the window and was surprised to see my dad slumped over the lawnmower, crying his eyes out.

I asked my mum, "What's up with him?"

"Oh," she said. "He's just going through a rough patch."

———

What do you call a polar bear in the jungle?

Lost.

What do you call a horny square?

An erectangle.

_____

I asked my German friend if he knew the square root of 81.

He said, *"Nein."*

We only bought this bottle of wine yesterday. Why is it half empty?

Maybe it's because you're a pessimist.

There are four quarters in
the Superbowl.

And that's why they brought out
50 Cent at half-time.

What are the two steps to marrying
a country girl?

First: a tractor.

Next: fertilizer.

Someone complimented me on my driving the other day. They left a note on my windshield.

It said: "Parking fine".

———————

Why do nurses always carry a red pen with them?

In case they need to draw blood.

Why did doctors name them haemorrhoids?

Asteroids was taken.

_____

What do you call a sleepy relative?

Nap-kin.

I met a ventriloquist
at a bar who told
me I was attractive.

I wasn't sure if
it was her or the
beer talking.

**What is as big as a hippopotamus
but weighs nothing at all?**

A hippopotamus's shadow.

_____

**What do you call a crocodile
that loves guacamole?**

A guacodile.

I slept like a baby last night.

I woke up every two hours and cried.

———————

My partner threatened to leave
me because of my obsession
with optical illusions.

I said, "Wait! This isn't what
you think it is!"

My mum told me to go the shop.
She said, "Get one carton of milk
and if they have avocados, get six."

When I got back, she looked at
what I'd bought.

"Why did you buy six cartons of milk?"
she asked.

I replied, "Because they had avocados."

What is muffins spelled backwards?

Exactly what you do when you take
them out the oven.

How much do dumplings weigh?

Wonton.

_____

Why did the baker's wife divorce him?

Because he was too kneady.

@DadSaysJokes is a community-run dad jokes network on Instagram, Facebook and Twitter, with over 5 million collective followers, inspired by the daily jokes of author Kit Chilvers' dad, Andrew.

Every day, followers submit their jokes and the team picks their favourites – or Dad just drops in his own zinger!

Kit, a young social networking influencer, started his career at the tender age of 14, when he created his original platform, Football.Newz. He has since added another fourteen platforms, including @PubityPets and monster meme Instagram page @Pubity, which has over 31 million followers.

Also available:

 @DadSaysJokes

 @Dadsaysjokes

 @DadSaysJokes